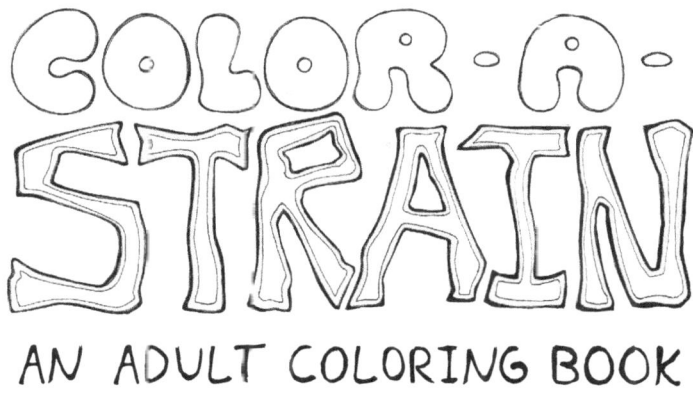

# AN ADULT COLORING BOOK

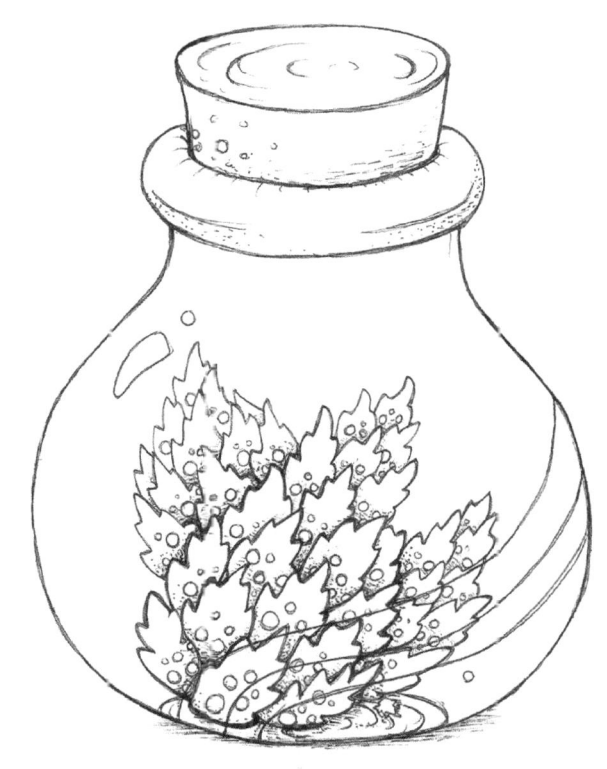

CREATED BY:

## NATHAN STAPLETON-MᶜKINZIE

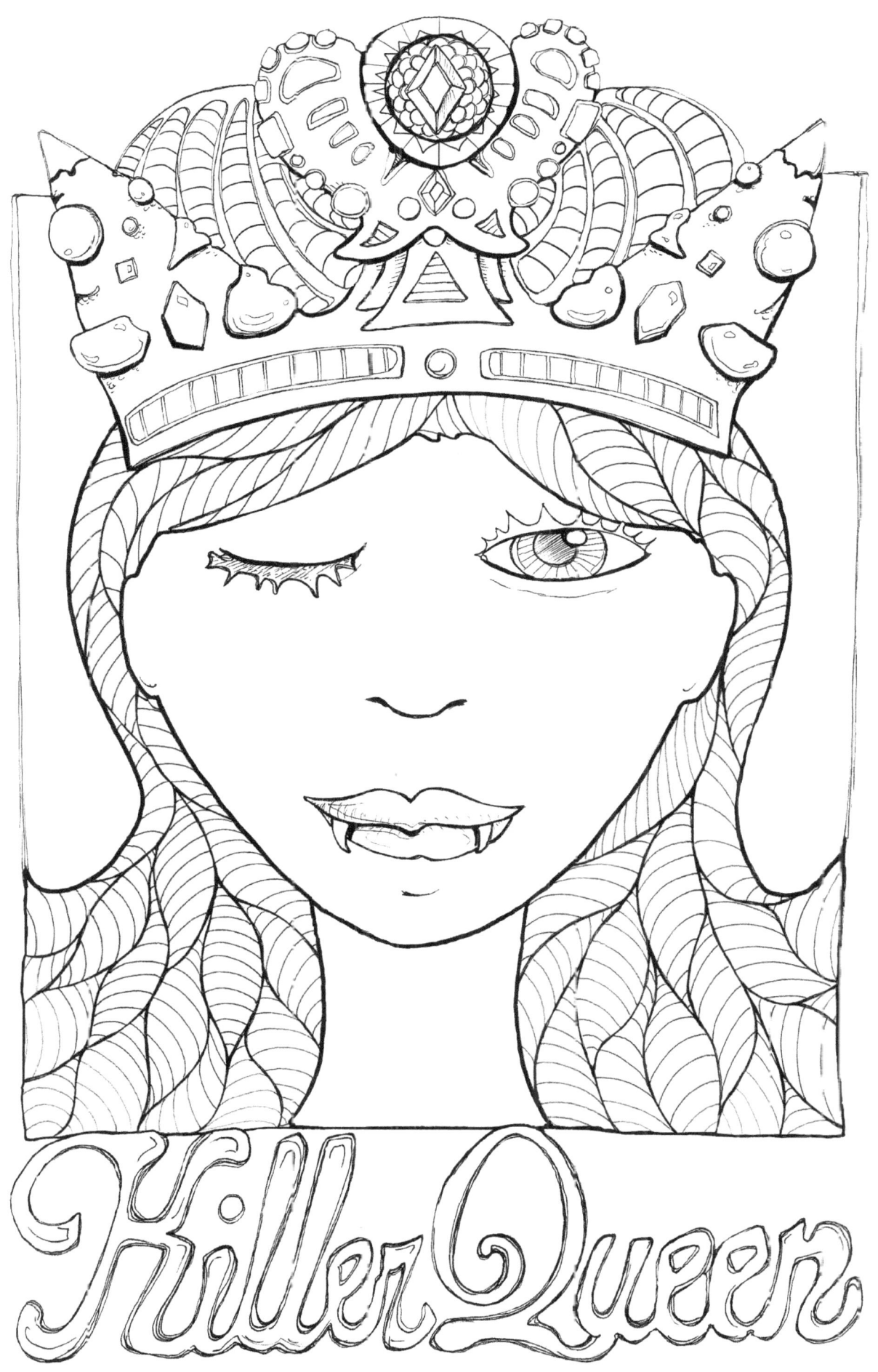

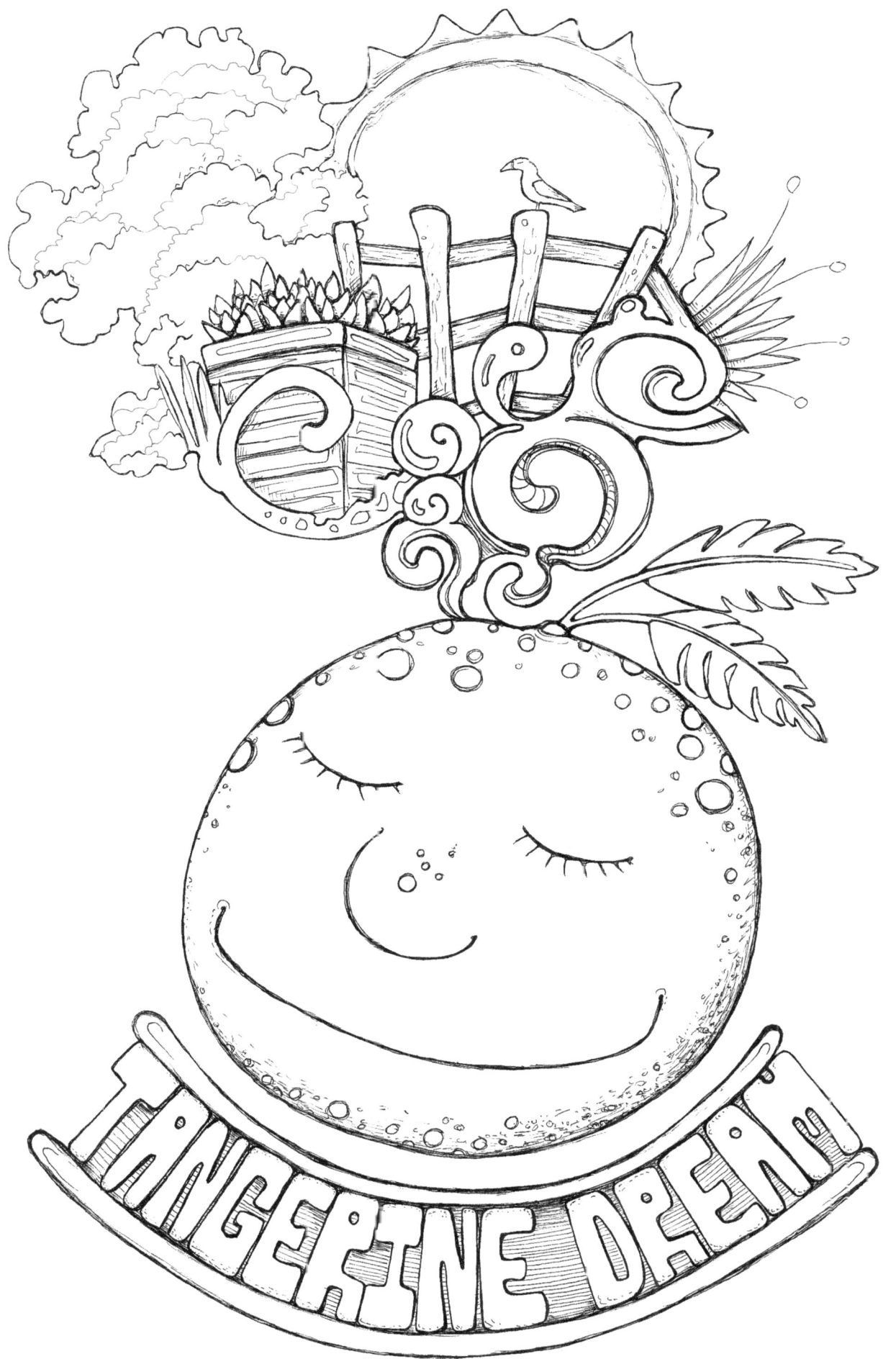

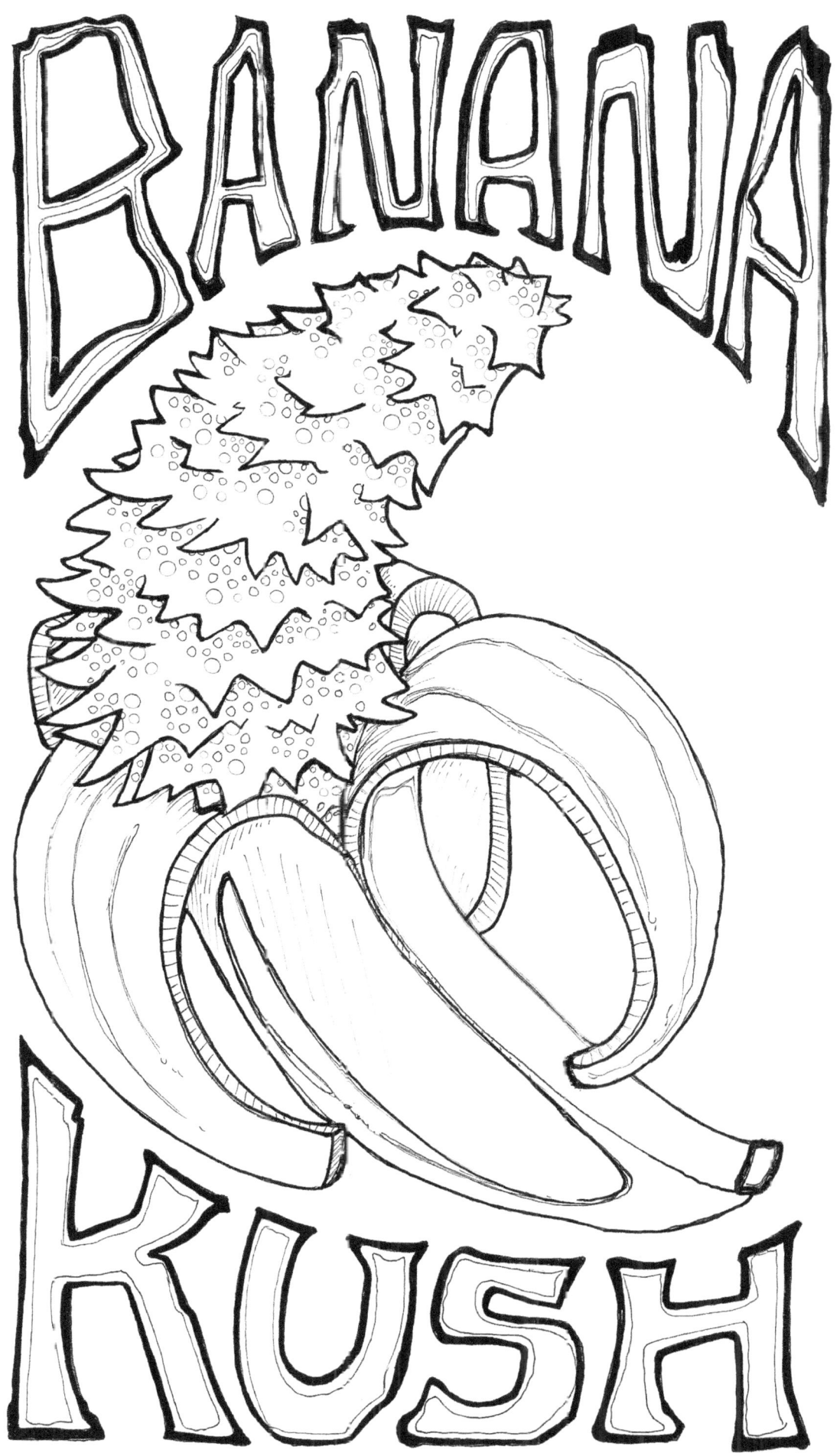

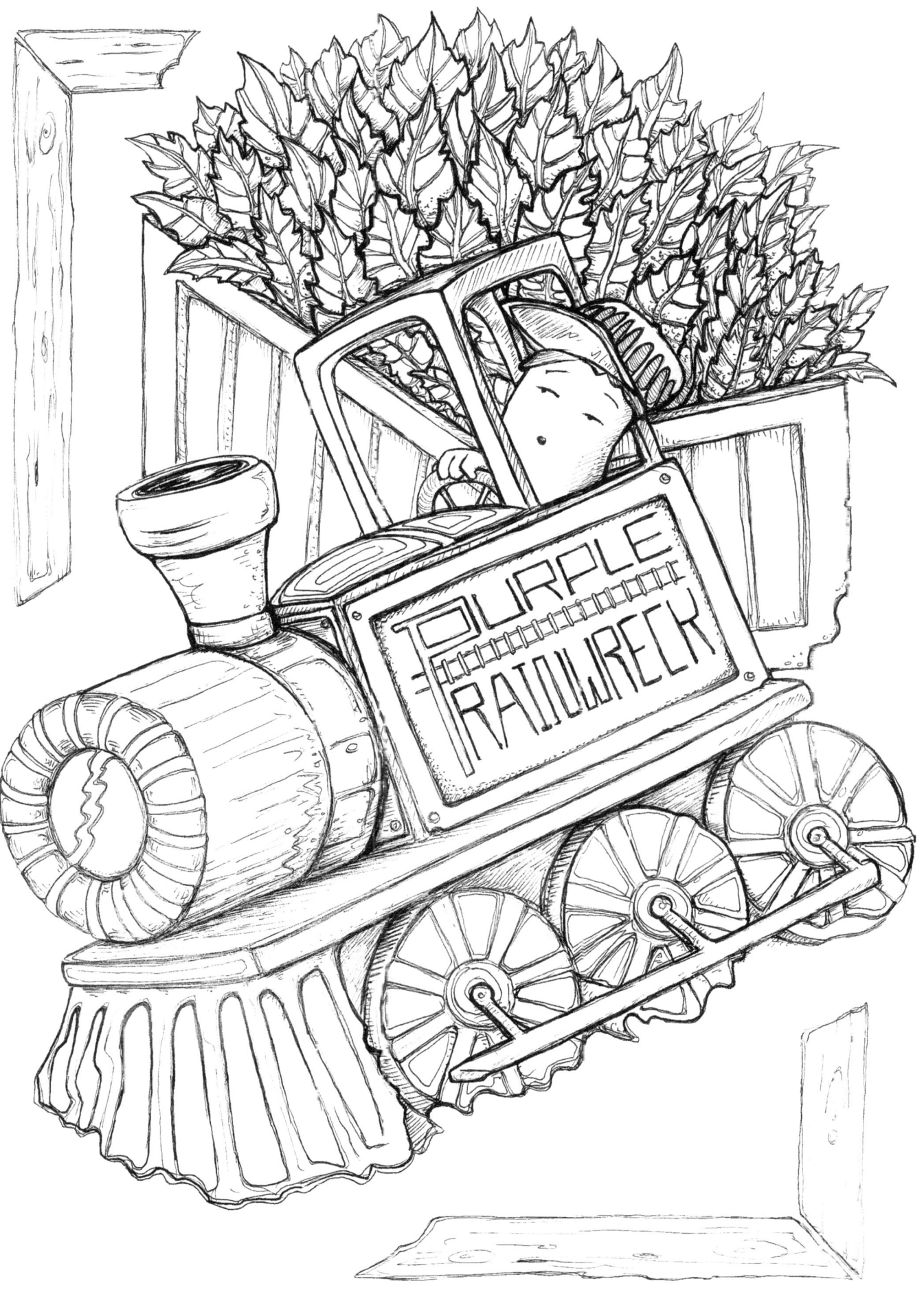

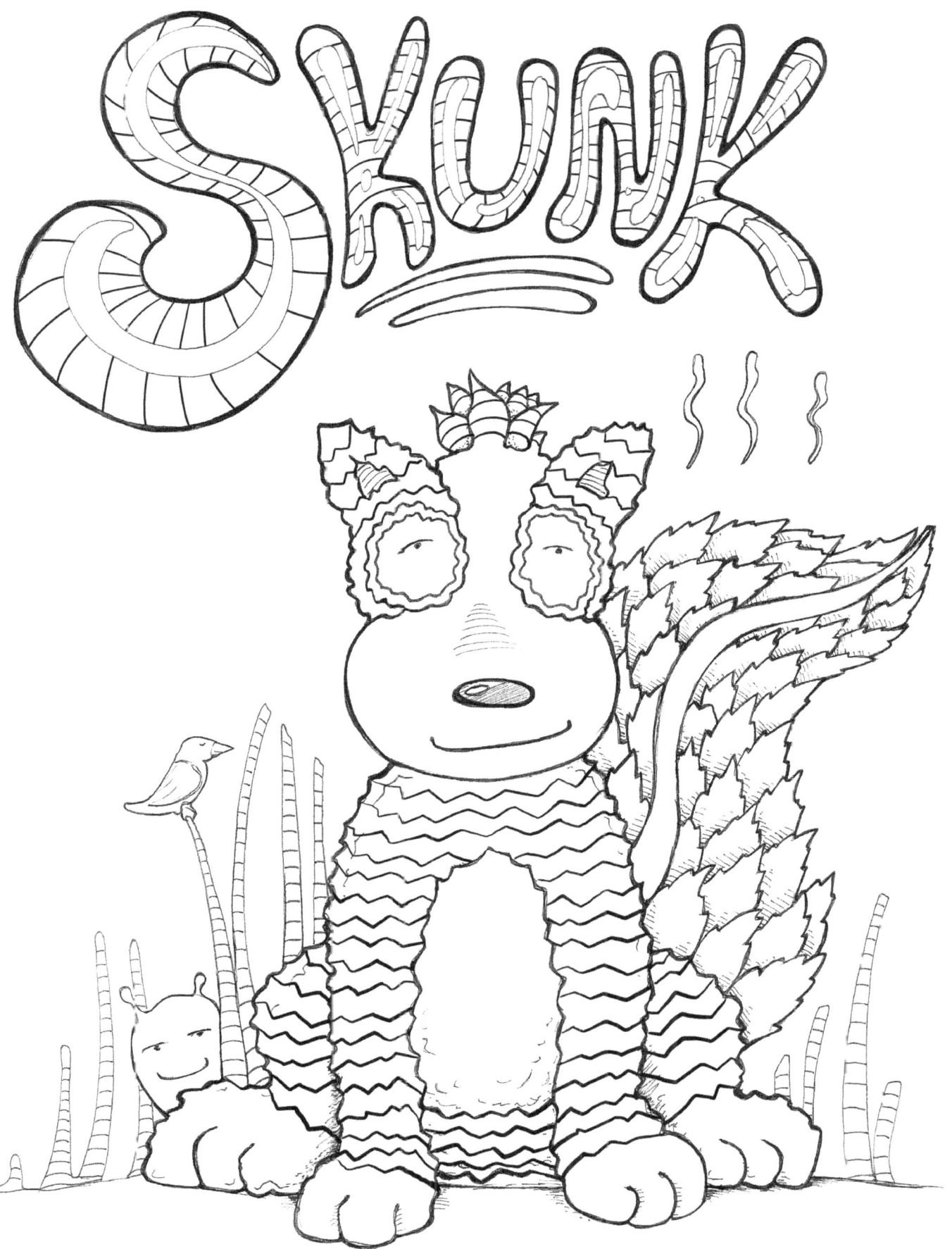

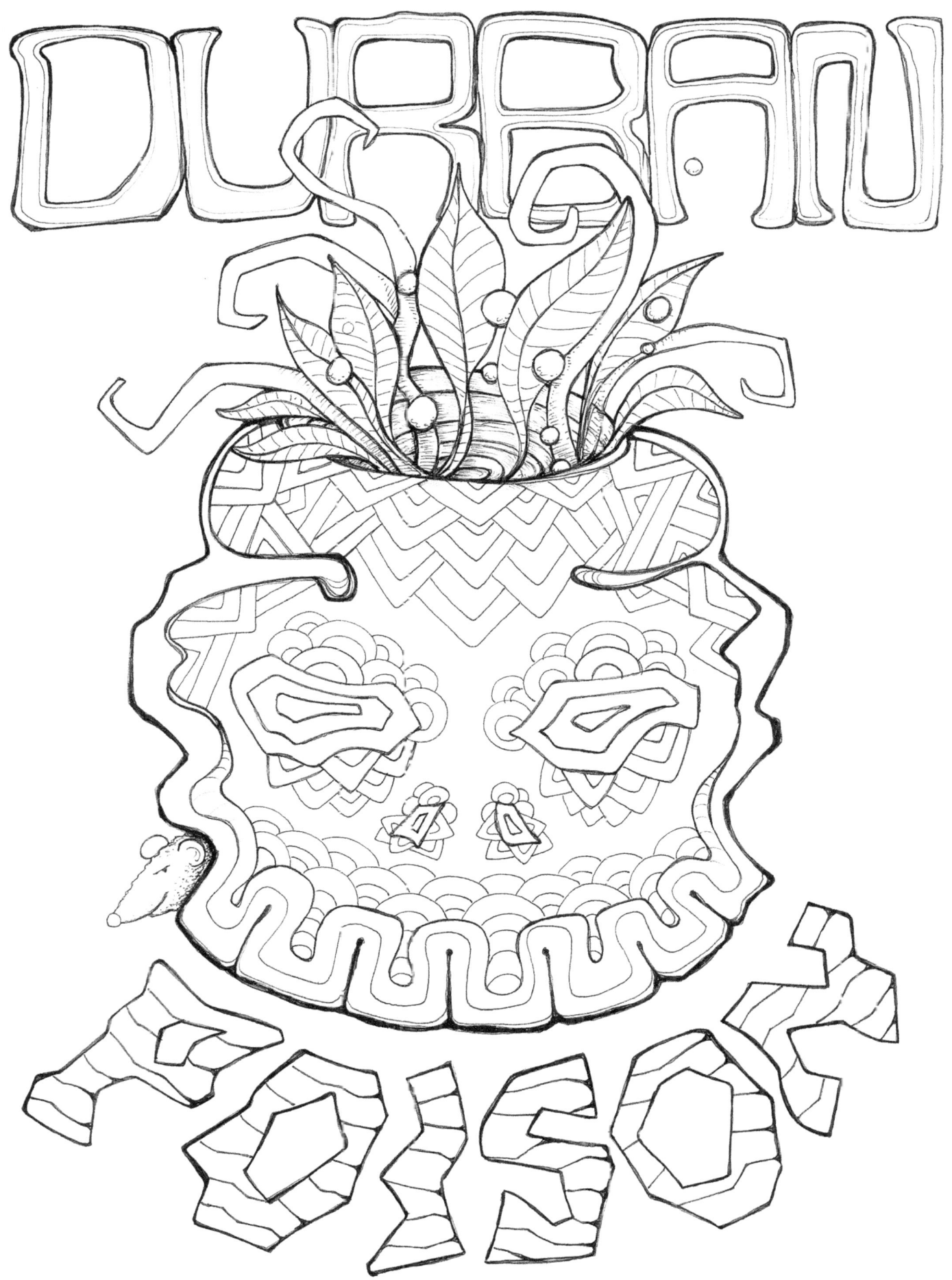

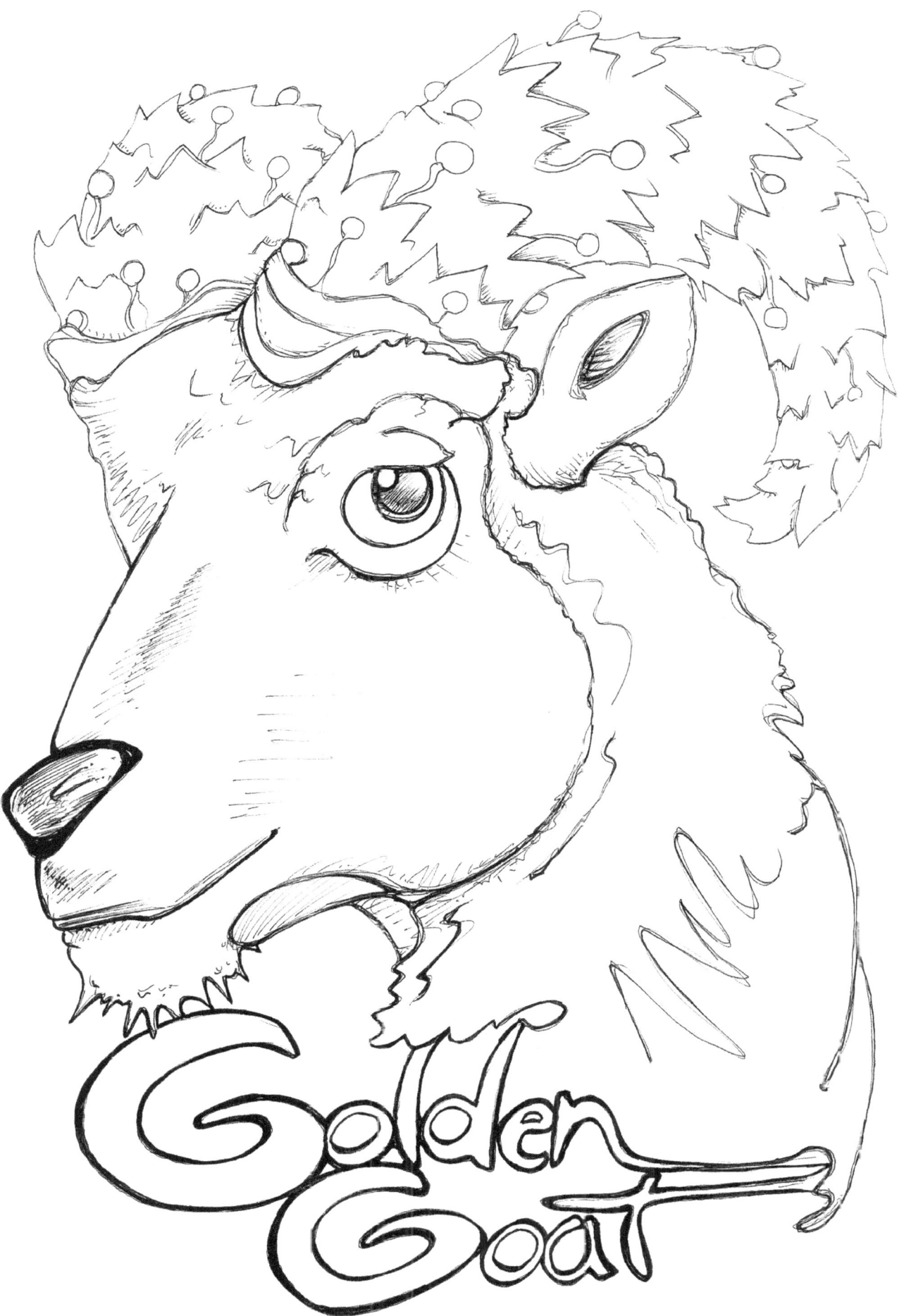

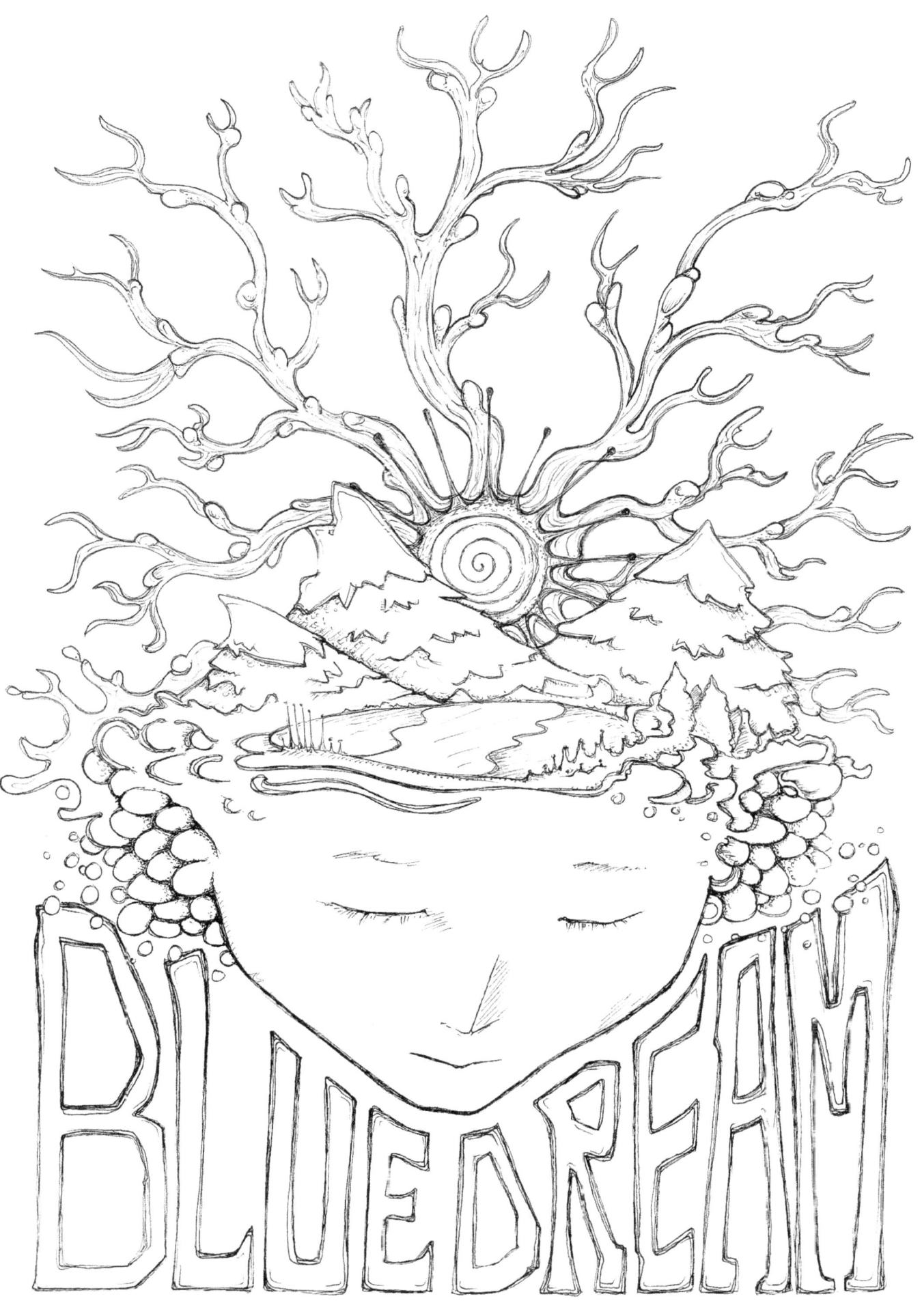

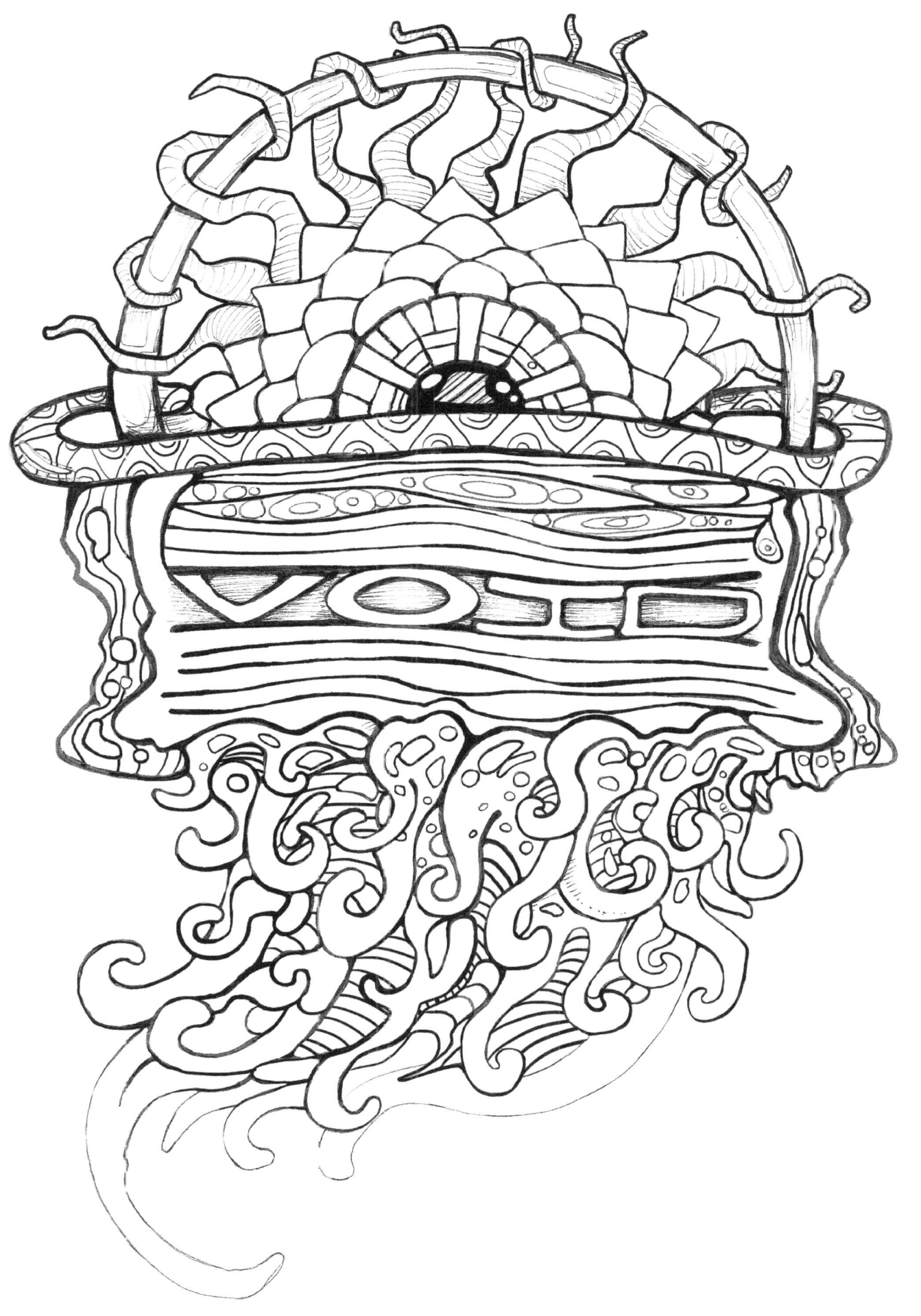

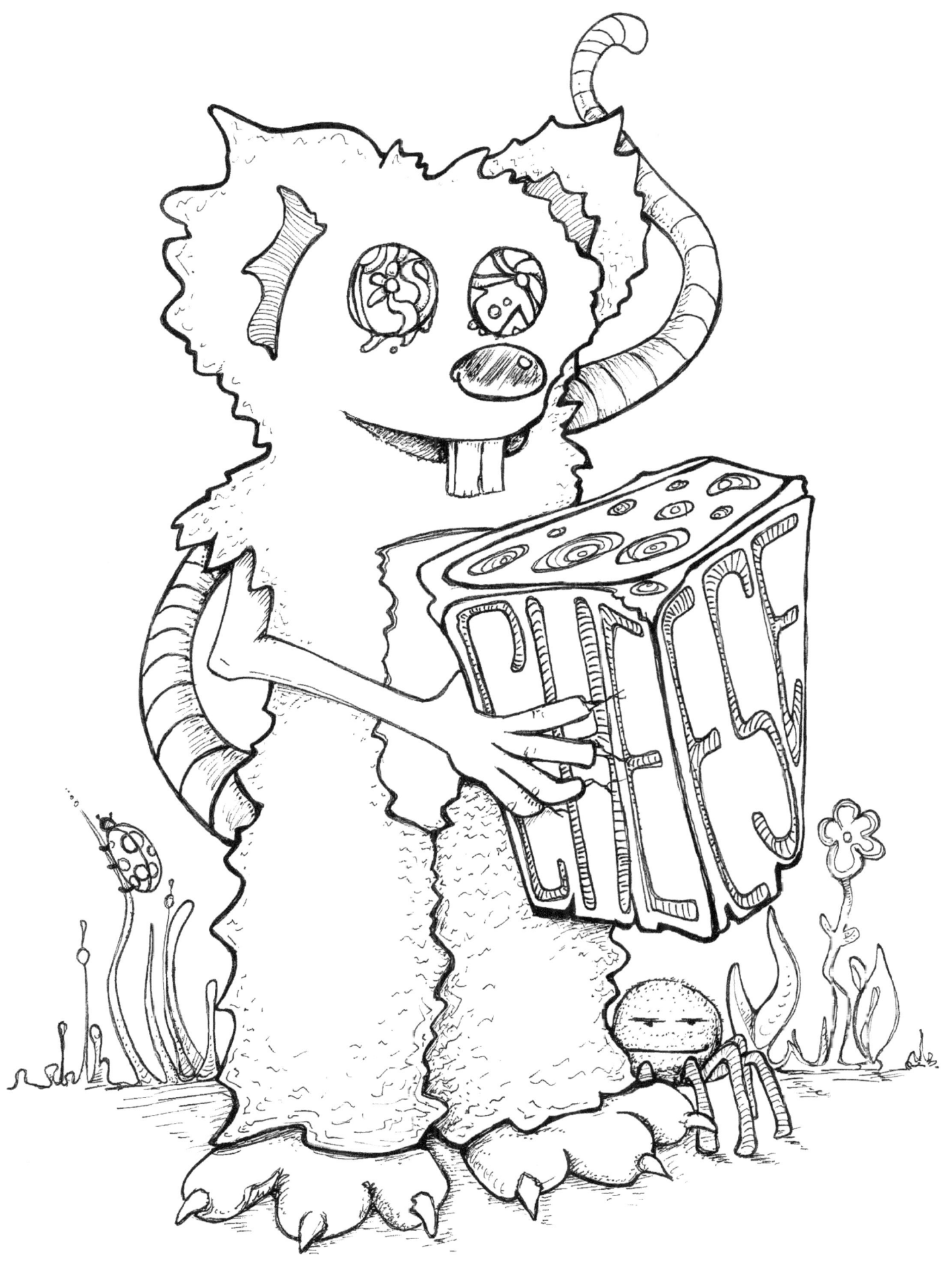

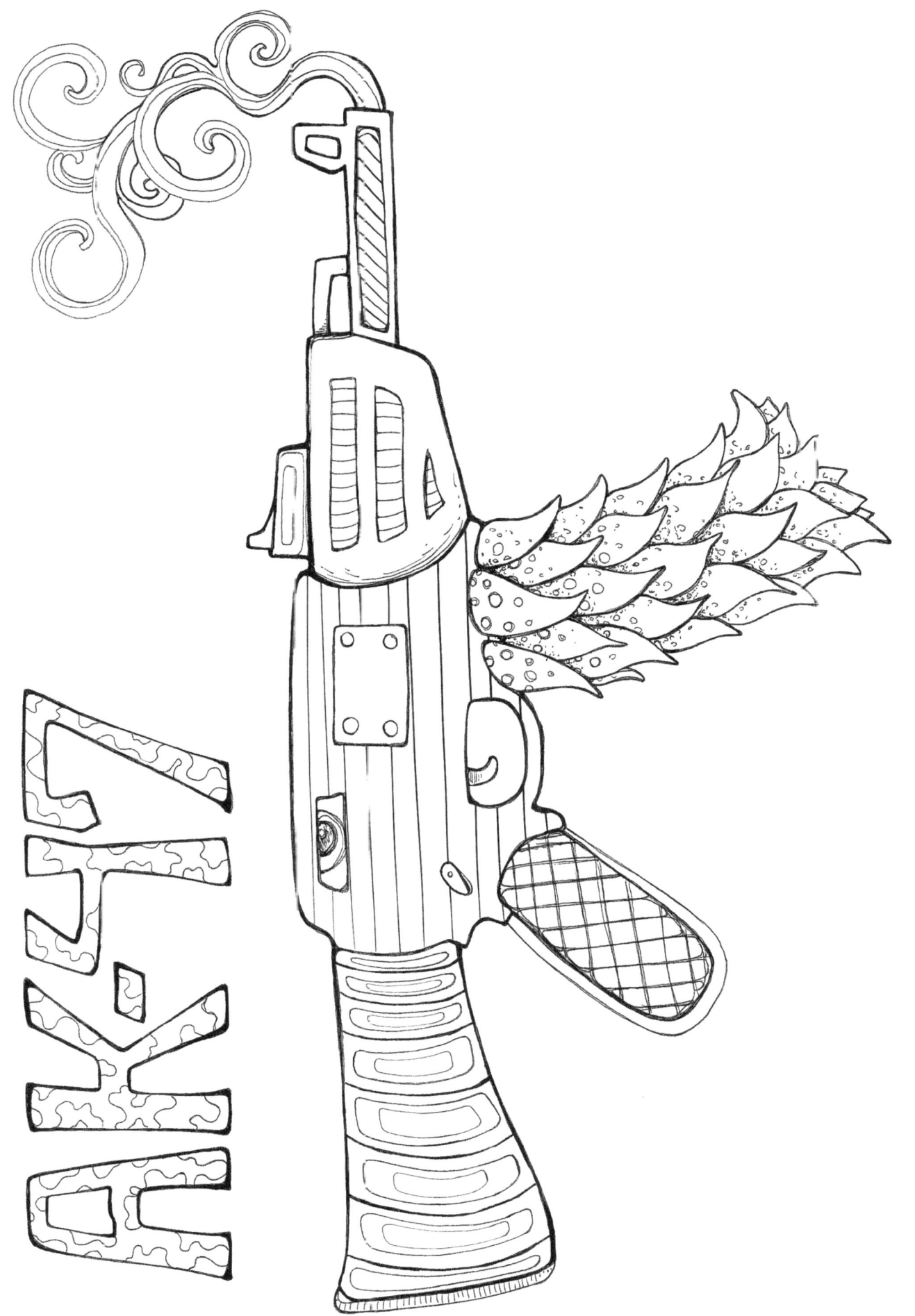

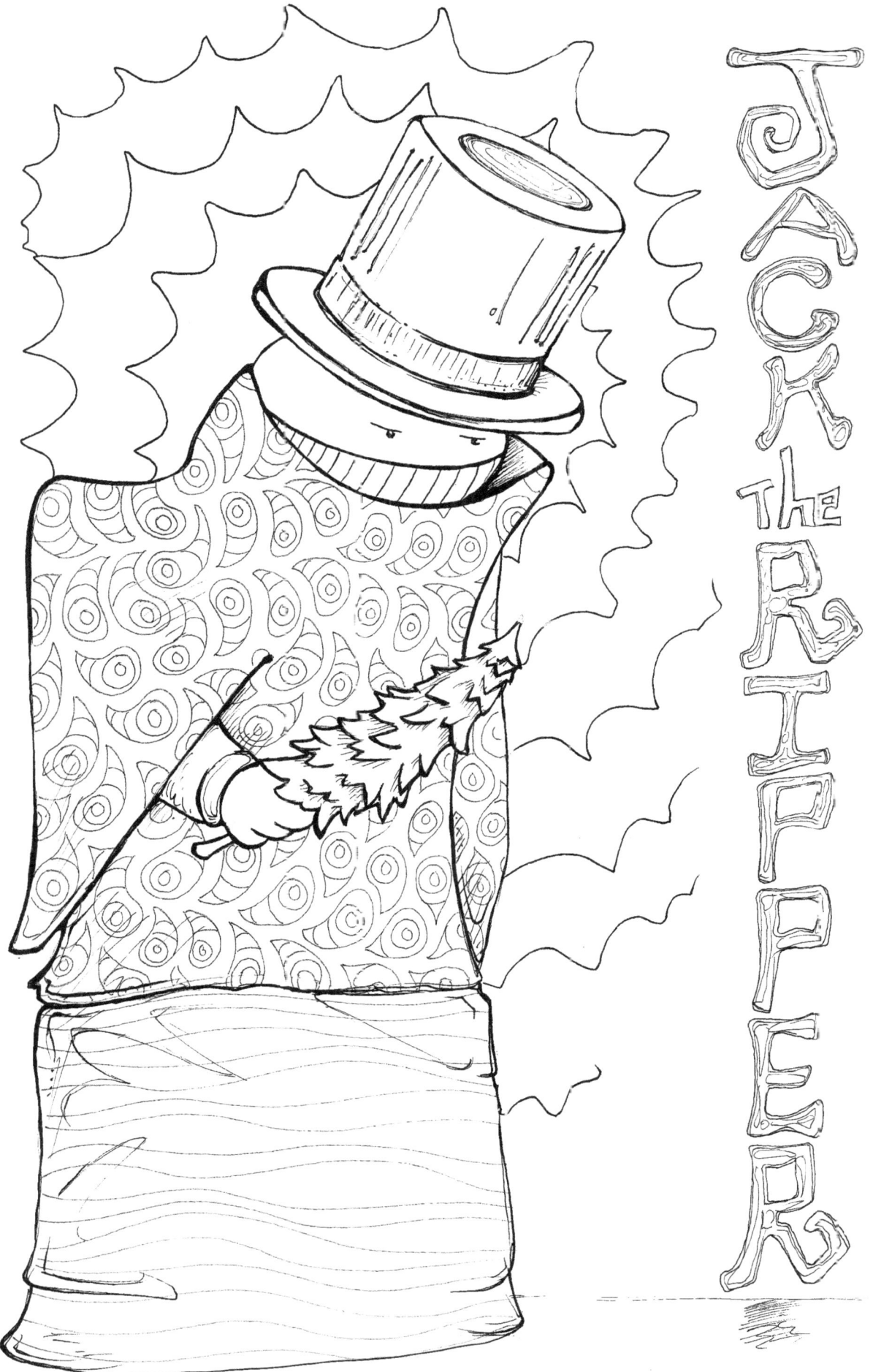

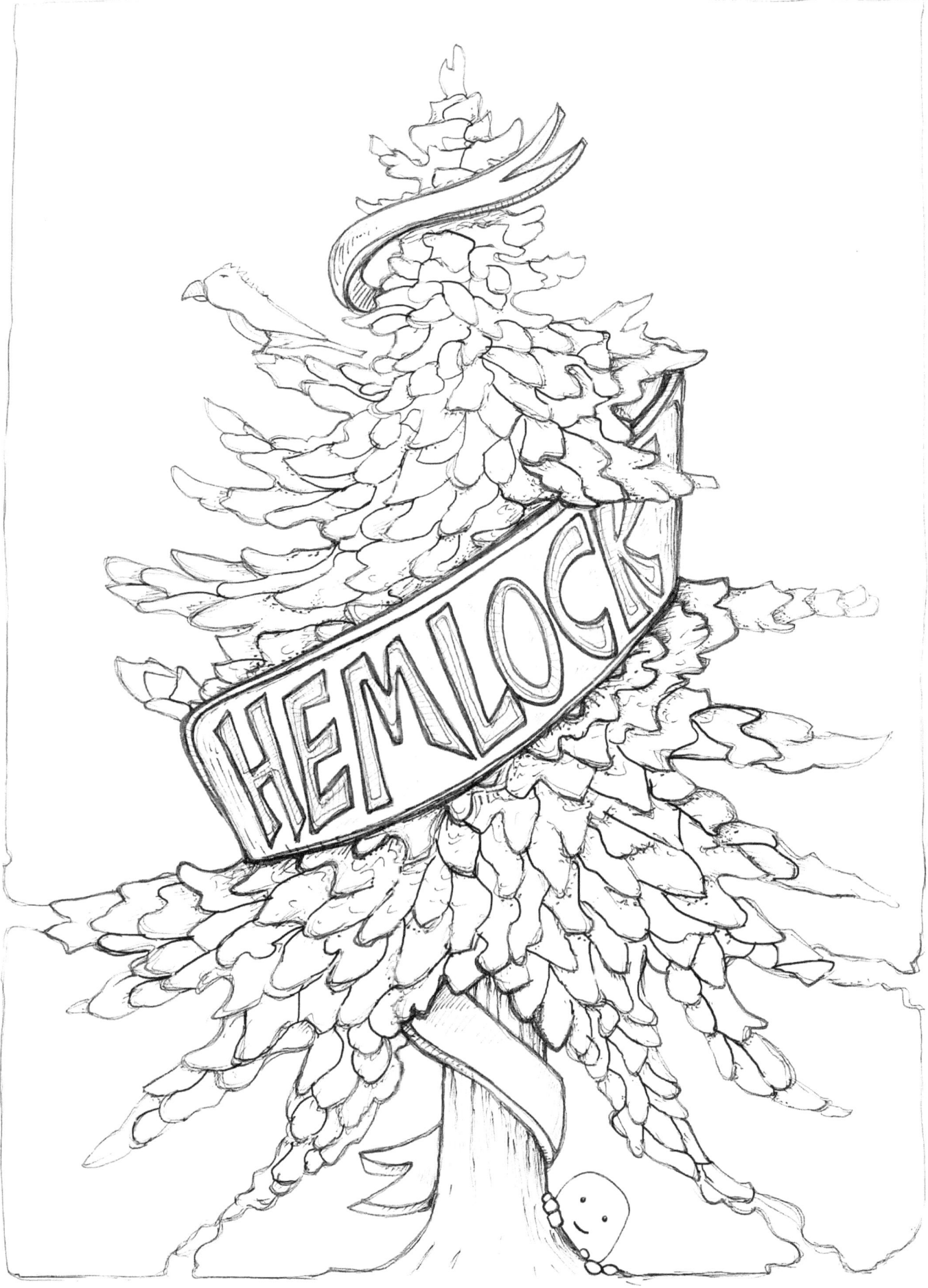

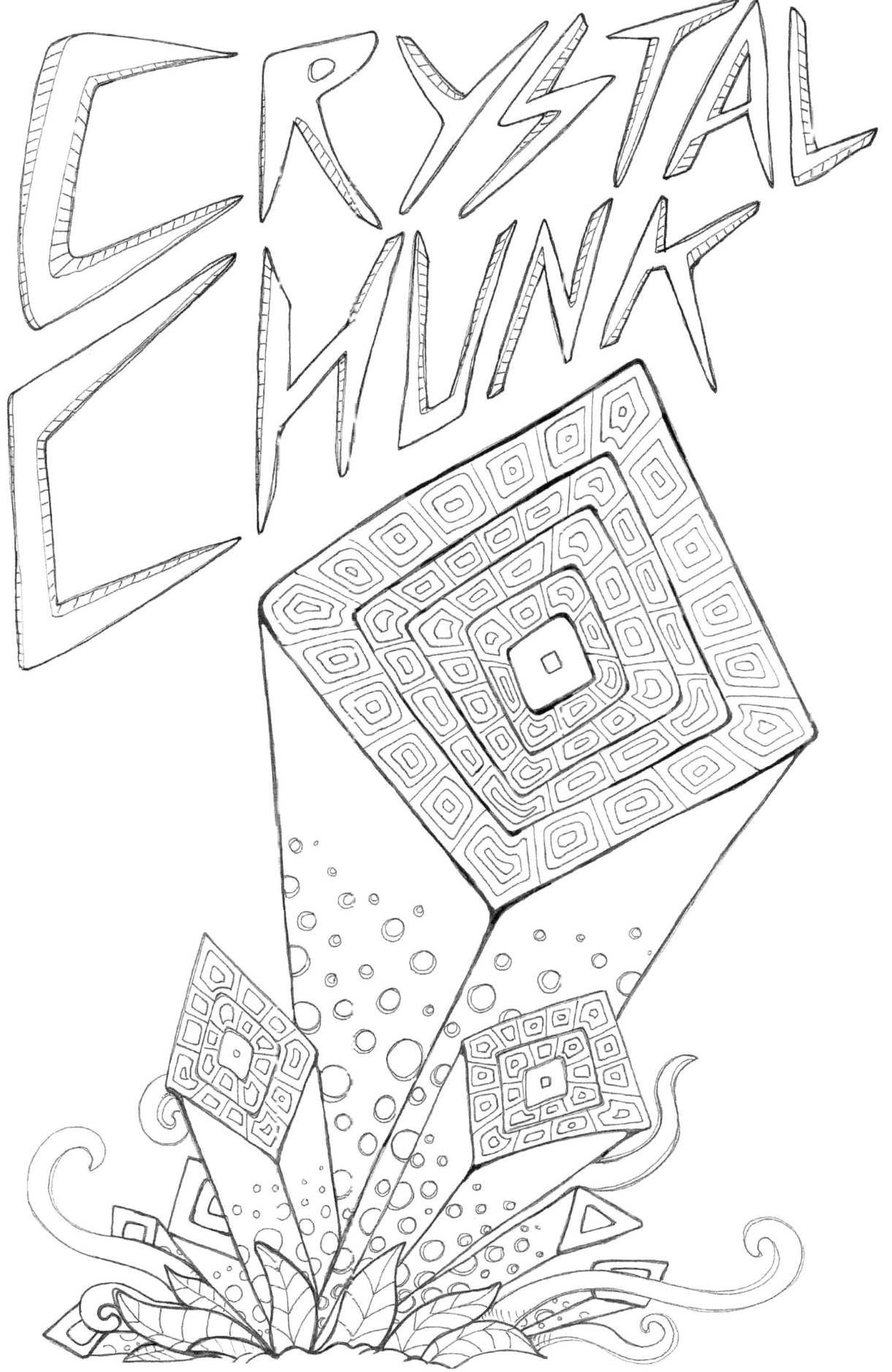

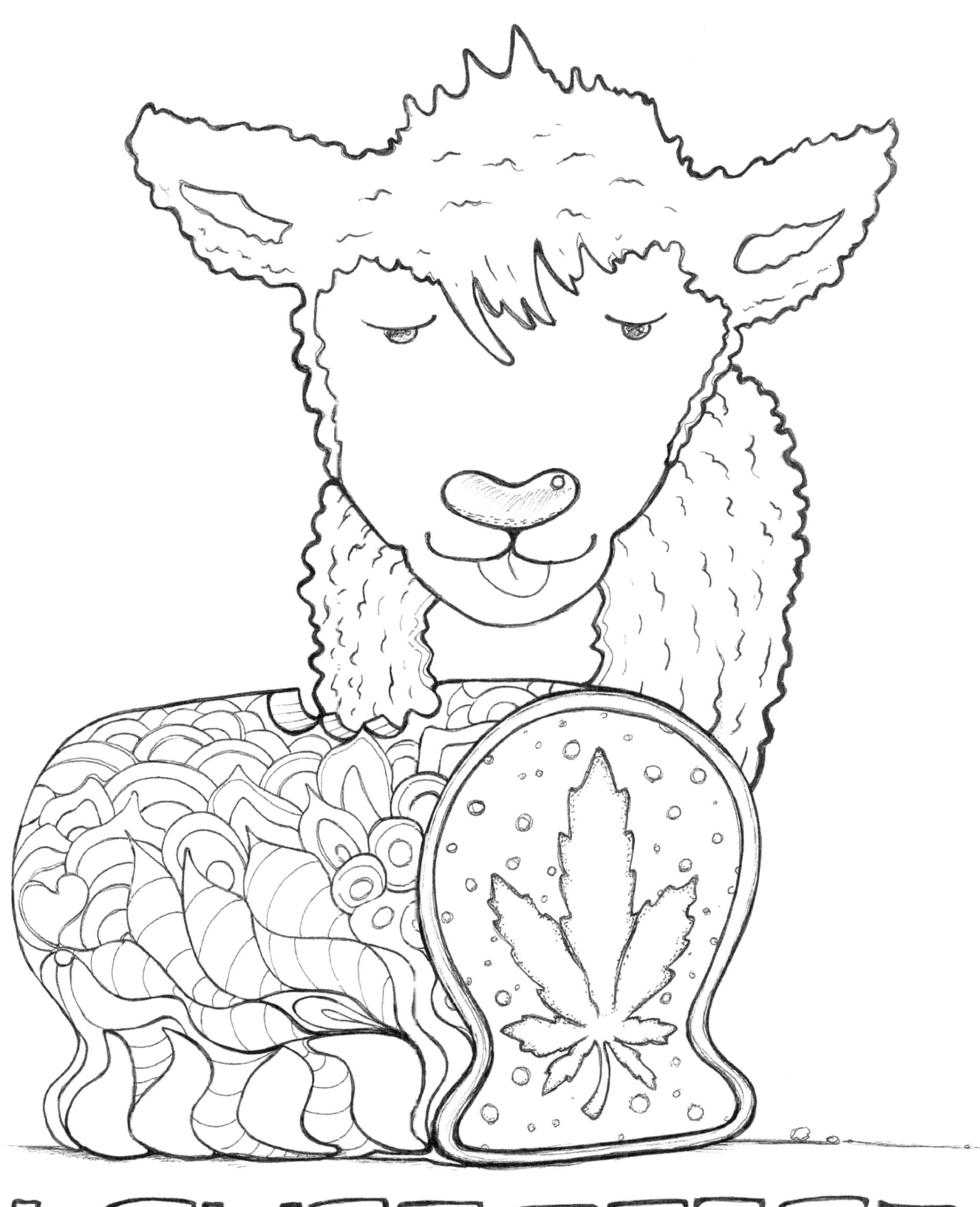

LAMBS BREAD

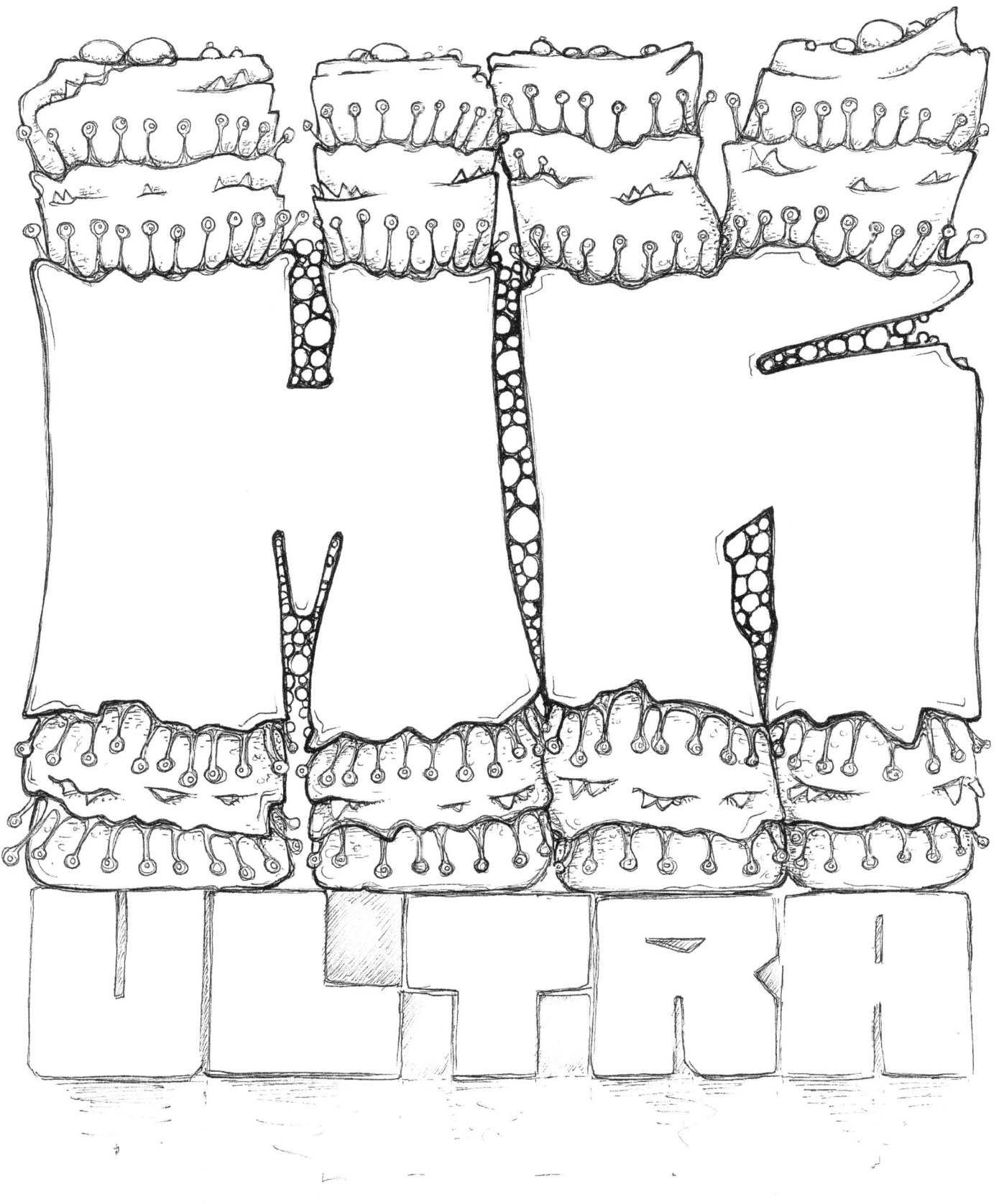

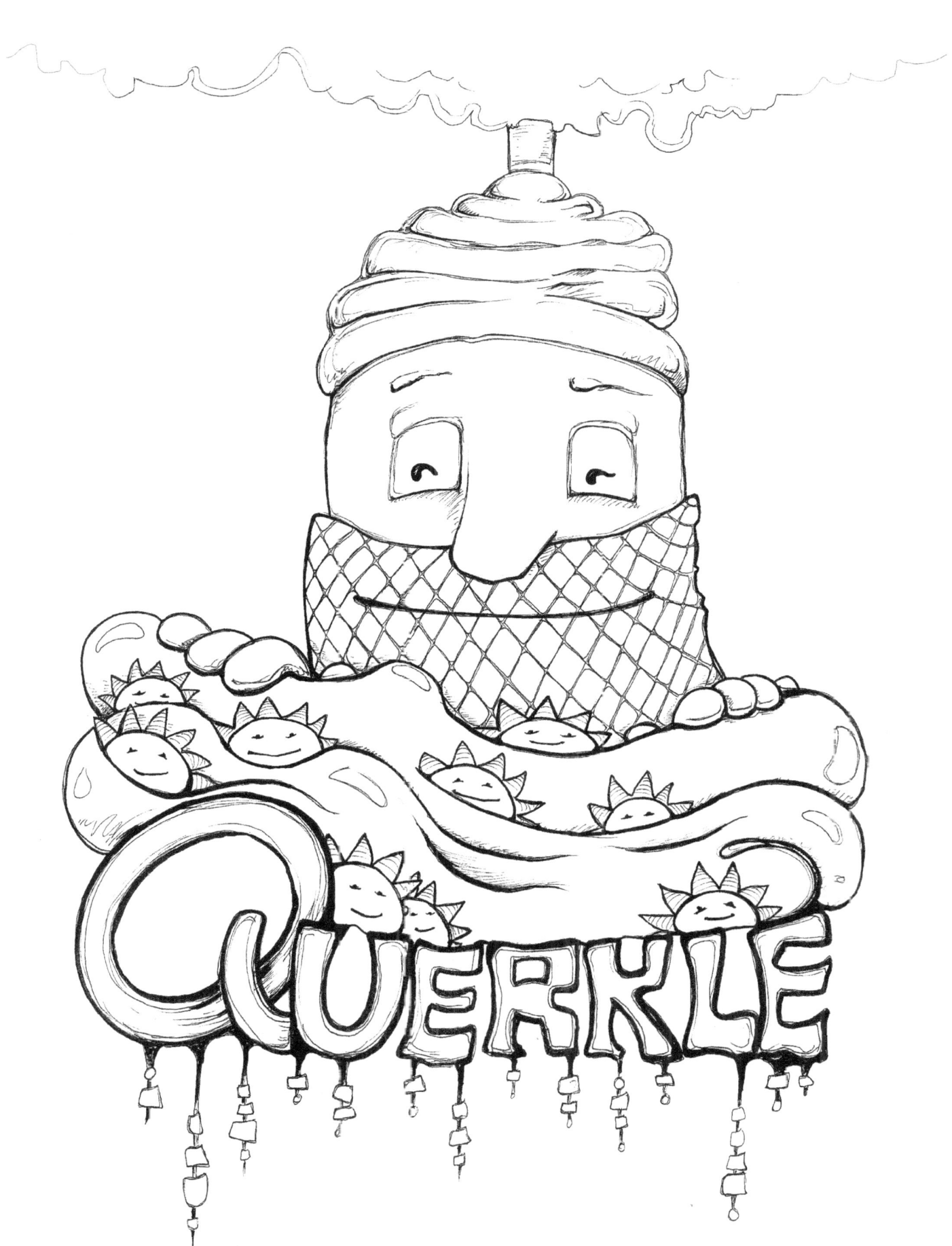

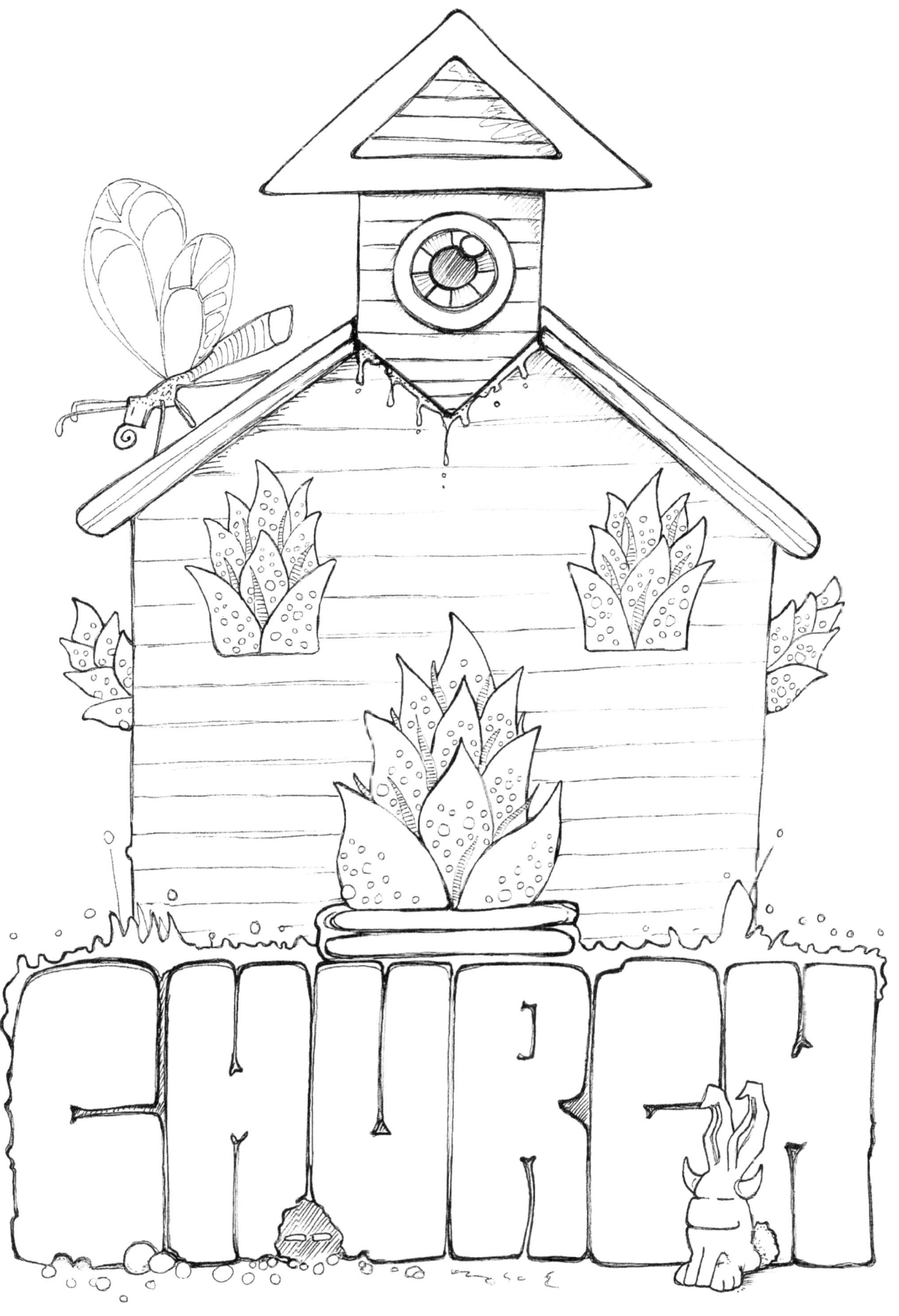

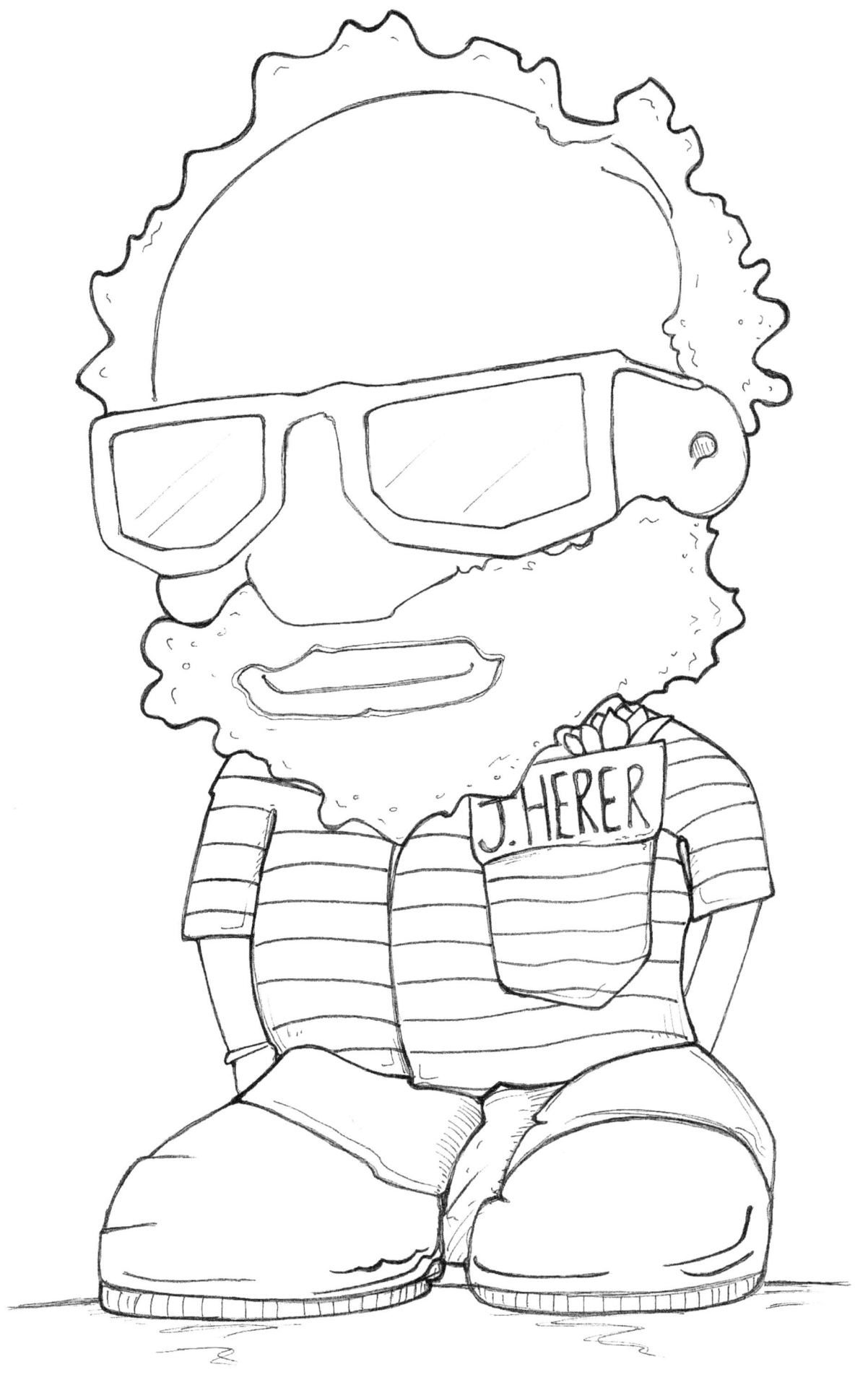

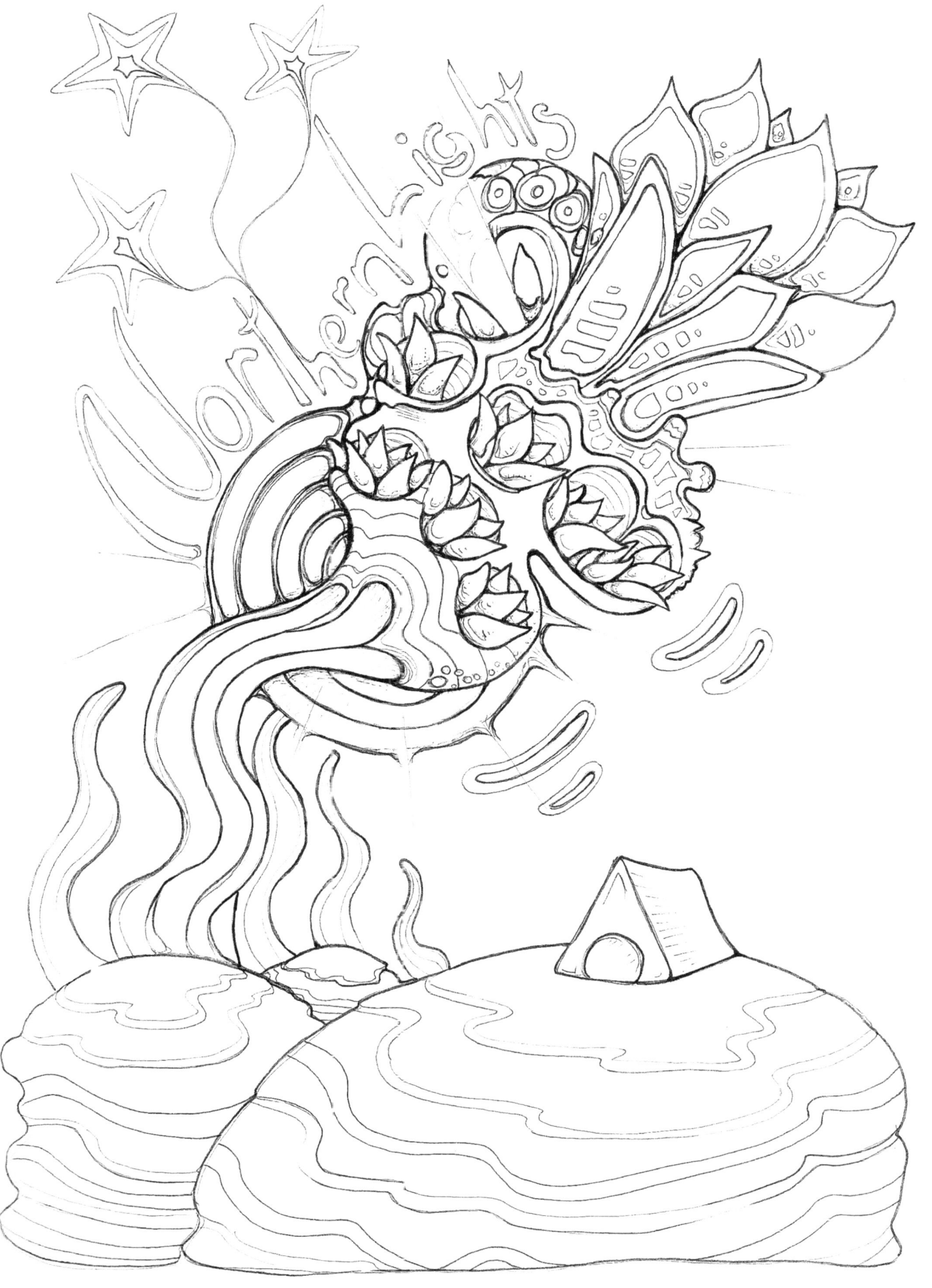

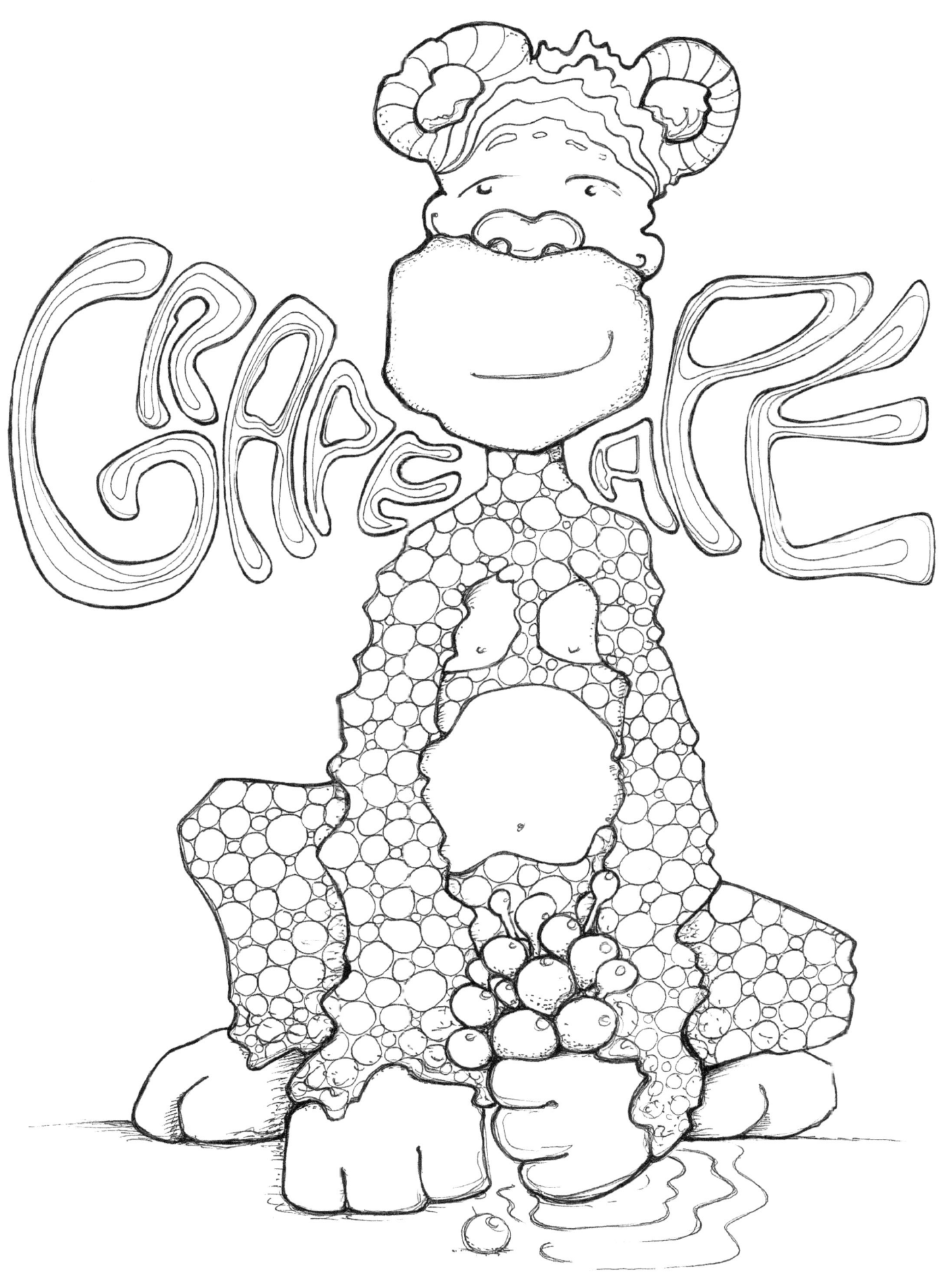

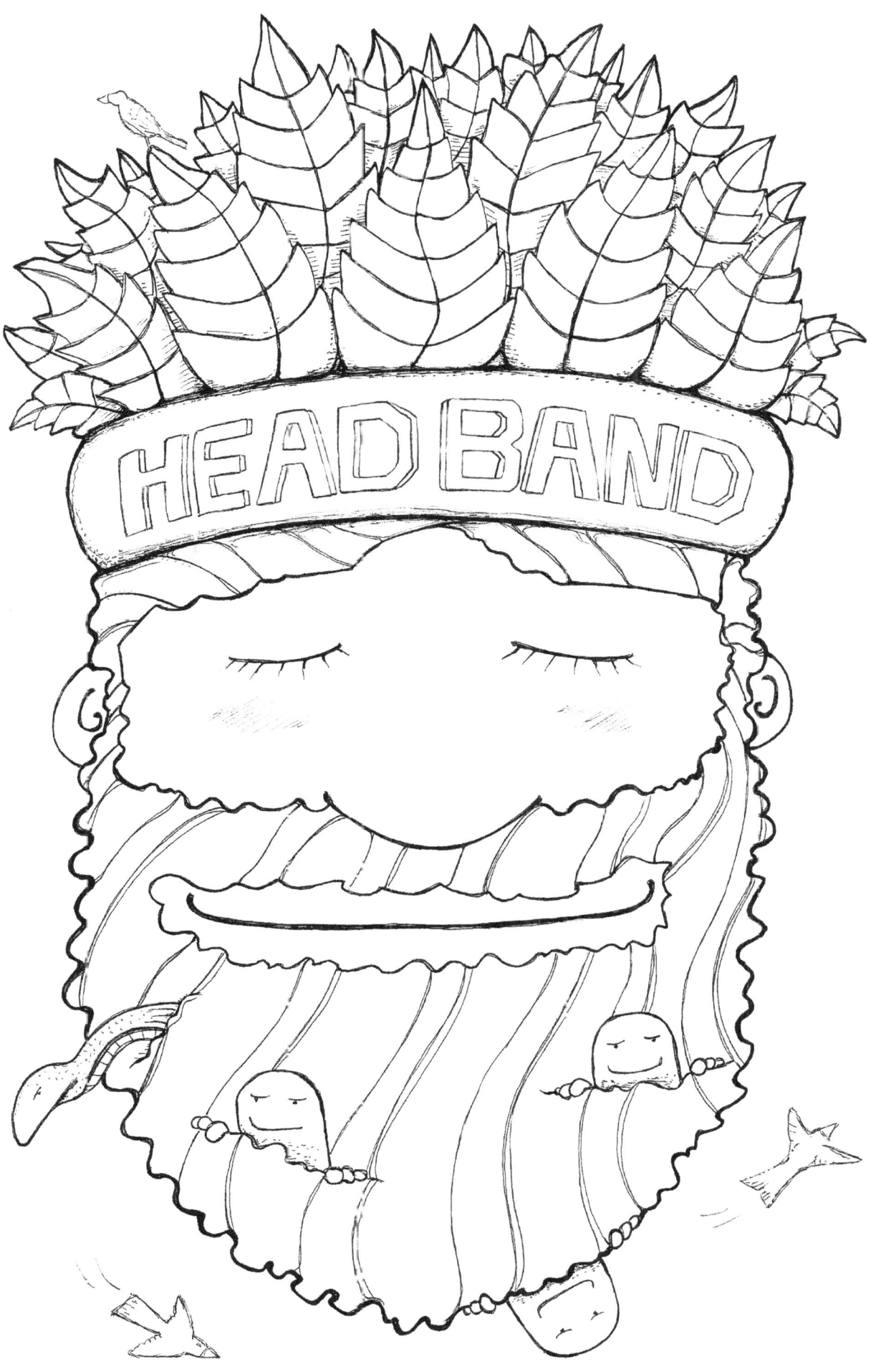

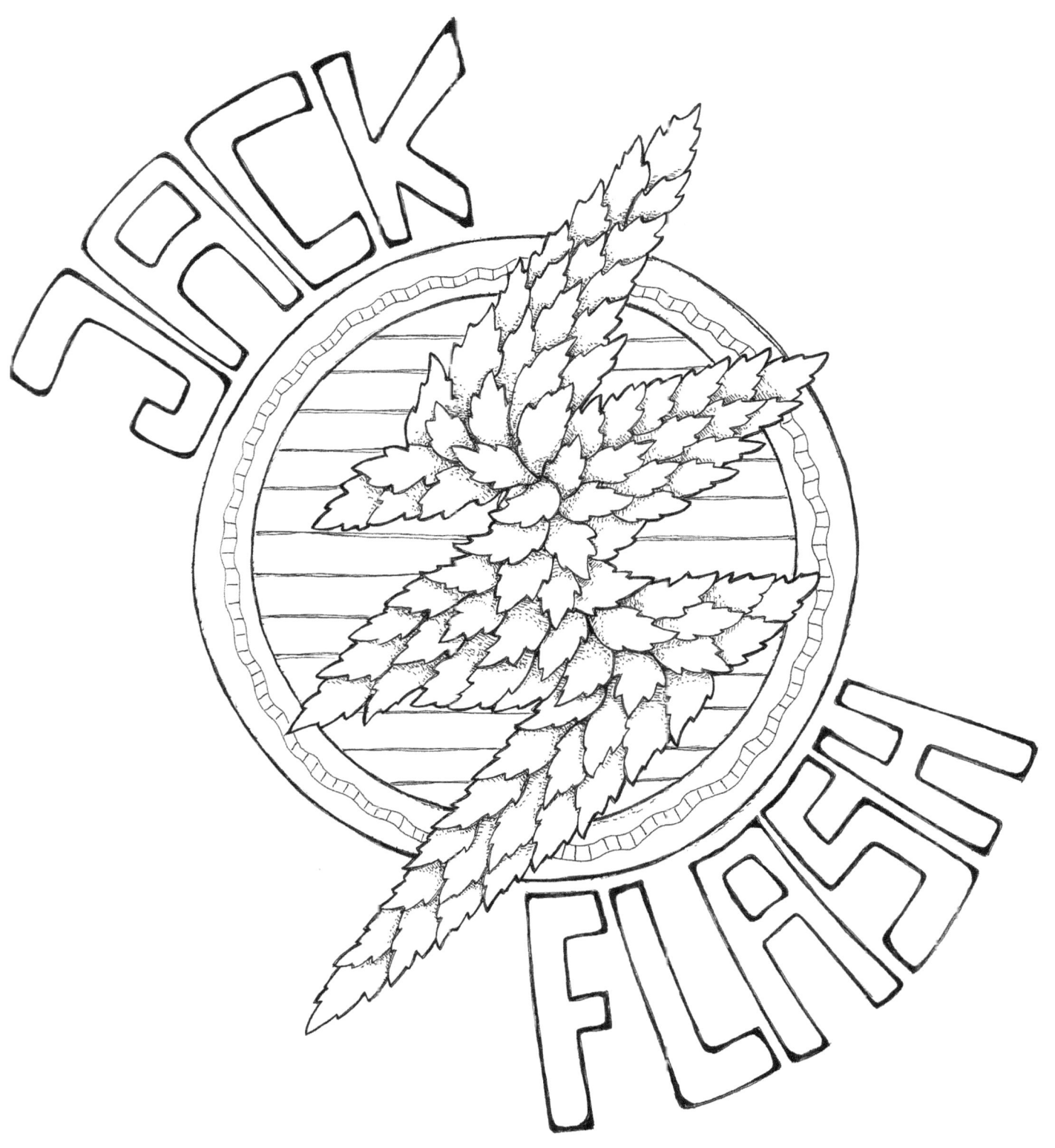

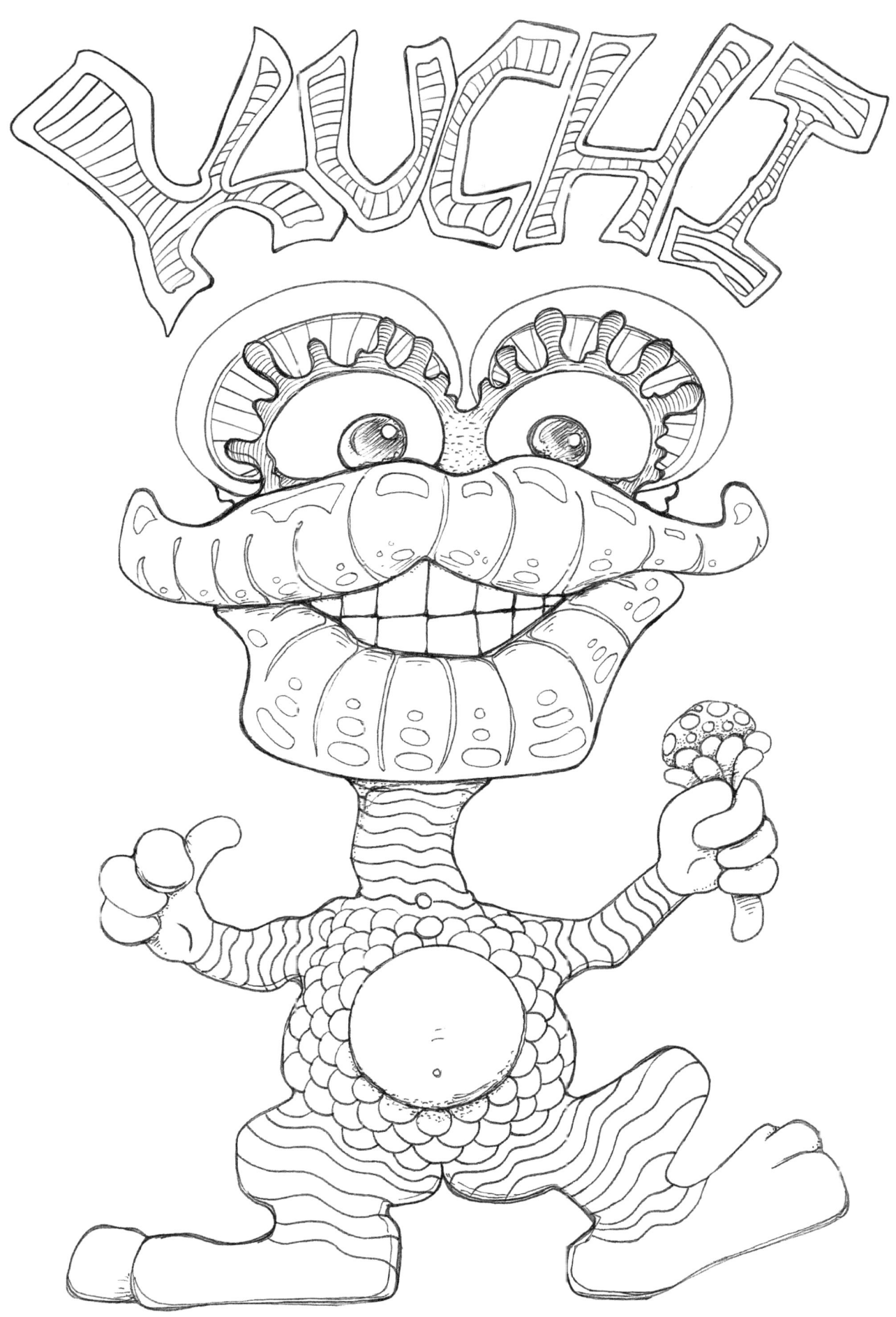

White Widow

www.ingramcontent.com/pod-product-compliance
Lightning Source LLC
Chambersburg PA
CBHW080601190526
45169CB00007B/2841